Wonderings of a Wanderer

Steve Gonzales jr

BookLeaf Publishing

India | USA | UK

Wonderings of a Wanderer © 2023 Steve Gonzales jr

All rights reserved.

No part of this publication may be reproduced, stored in a retrieval system, or transmitted, in any form or by any means, electronic, mechanical, photocopying, recording or otherwise, without the prior written permission of the presenters.

Steve Gonzales jr asserts the moral right to be identified as author of this work.

Presentation by *BookLeaf Publishing*

Web: www.bookleafpub.com

E-mail: info@bookleafpub.com

ISBN: 9789358317510

First edition 2023

Awoken

Do not ask my age, for that is just a
number.
Restrain from questioning my education,
it is only a degree.
Ask not where I am from, it is only a
place.
Abstain thoughts of knowing who I
am,unless we have spoken.
My home is wherever I lay my head
when it is time for slumber.
My mind is only a portion of me.
I am made up of the experiences that
make me awoken.

Standing on the moon

Standing on the moon I can see earth in the distance.
 In it are all the places and people I've ever known.
  Standing on the moon I am weightless.
   Yet i feel heavy thinking of somewhere I long to be.
   I am here in the vastness of space.
 But it means nothing if I'm all alone.
    Standing on the moon my spirit is so close to heaven though it's still restless.
  If you're down there & can hear my voice let I know that you are here with me.

My heart is a beach

My heart is a beach;
every now & then
things get swept away like footprints in the sand.
Memories of scenes are scattered far & wide
similar to seashells.
At times my mood changes in the way music
plays on a radio.
It has beauty that not everyone stops to see
yet continuously happens just as rising & setting
of sun.
There's people who tip toe that only get so far
then others who stoke flames of the bonfire.

Hope

When the road feels long
thoughts of her keep me going.
If something happens that
doesn't make sense thinking
about her reminds me to
believe. Time shall pass yet
how I feel for her won't
change. She is proof that
anything is possible when the
world so easily wants to tell
me no & nope. Life is full of
uncertainty but she is someone
I have the gift of knowing. Her
belief in me encourages me to
constantly dream & achieve.
When other people see things
one way she helps me see them
differently which to some might
seem strange. All these reasons
& more are I why I love hope.

Made me

When the world feels to heavy, let me remind myself it's not mine to carry. If I get lost on my way, let me remember that unseen paths make for new way.In moments of confusion let me recall that it's ok learn as I'm going. As sky grows dark for a night let me revive thoughts how in daytime the sun shines for me. If the path has unexpected scenes let me recollect it has happened before & it doesn't have to be scary. In situations When life doesn't go as I expected let me recognize on how that could end up okay. So may I eyes be fully open to let me see what's out there while I'm exploring. When I have reached the end of my journey let I scatter my spirit in all the places that together made me.

live, love & play!

My world has changed & it can't go back to how it was; so I must find a way to keep going forward. For I too am not how I was before, thus it'll be a new me in a different reality. If you knew me prior please have patience as I am trying to adapt to the change. If you meet me in the now keep in mind that I am a work in progress still trying to figure things out. If we meet in the future know that experiences have made into the man who you see today. To all of you I say don't know what will happen but I'm doing my best to keep going onward. All that being said let us enjoy life while we can yet always keep in our hearts those who are in eternity. I don't know about all of you but me I don't want just normal, I want to explore & even experience the strange. As I am out there living & finding what life is about. As a result my philosophy is live, love & play!

I'm giving up

I'm giving up my worries.
Going to believe everything will turn out
alright in time.
I'm giving up my stress.
Knowing there's some things I can't
control.
I'm giving up my anger.
Since nothing is worth my peace.
I'm giving up my fear.
Instead l'Il live my life in the moment.
So when my days are done I have
stories.
That are sublime.
Maybe others won't understand but
to me they'll be priceless.
To my friends, family,God & good
vibes I'Il hold.
The journey won't be easy cause in
life there's always some danger.
Yet starting right now all negative
energy I release.
Trusting my vision will be made
Clear.
& I will be quiet when needed
knowing messages come to those who
are silent.

Still dream

In a world where so many people are losing their humanity I am trying to stay human. In a time that everyone is rushing from one place to the next I am looking for a quieter route. In a universe that's full of telescopes facing the sky I am trying to stay grounded. In a era that individuals are becoming woke I still dream. Life has unexpected events but still I do the best that I can. There's so much to see everywhere I look & even more then can be figured out. I am no solider though I will fight for those like me if we are surrounded. Being this way makes me unlike others but who's the one who gets to deem.

Self improvement

Snow was scattered as far his eye could see.
Wind was heavy & wet as socks in boots as the
man trekked on.
Every step was slow moving yet it was
movement.
With his head held high, he set out into the
unknown.
He wasn't sure exactly what would find along
the way.
Just knew had to go out & explore.
Daylight was limited so had to make haste
since conditions were far from optimal.
Though that wouldn't deture his spirit & will.
Even when his body felt weak.
His sense of wanderlust kept him going even
when things seemed bleak
Because inside was desire that couldn't easily be
fill.
It was something so basic & primal.
something once tried, it was ever wanting taste
Making the explorer want more.
So he dared from start till the end of day.
This was the life he had chosen.
A way of working on self improvement.

Learning how to live fully yet proceed with caution.
I know all this because the man was me!

The Divine

There might be times that
you feel lost but remember a
river is always part the sea.
Clouds may roll in though the
sun's warmth is still felt. Sky
does at times darken yet which
is what allows the moon to
shine.
Life has unexpected
moments this can be good if let
it be.
Some times a whisper
says more than a yell. Never
forget that within you is same
energy in everything created by
The Divine.

Life is unpredictable

What good does it do to have a room full of candles if you don't strike a match? Tell me why do some people put on music if they're not going to dance? How come individuals lift the head if scared to open their eyes? Everyone's got an itch yet not all are going to scratch. We all get opportunities though some won't dare to take chance. You won't see new places if you're scared to explore cause you think might die. You can't find answers if you're not willing to search. You'll never make progress if refuse to make an effort to advance. Life is unpredictable but it's also for living so you might as well try.

Hold on

Hold on, when you start to feel not sure how much more can take; hold on one more night. Everything is going to be ok, despite what it seems like at moments like these when world seems dark. Just hold on; the sun will be here soon to help you see, so keep looking up. To some people the future is scarv but not those of who hold on, for we know that life will turn out ok if we keep holding on. Let our beliefs carry us through difficult times for we know that what we believe will help us hold on.

Brave soul

Brave soul your feathers might have been ruffled yet you can still fly. Brave soul your feet may hurt though you are still able to dance. Brave soul you might feel weak rest now so you'll regain your strength. Brave soul tonight your heart hurts but in time it will heal. Strong soul you can accomplish so much if you dare to try. Strong soul don't ever be scared to live & take a chance. Strong soul are going to make it through regardless of your journey's length. Strong soul always know your heart is beautiful regardless of you feel.

Dare to try

Would you dance if the only music was beating of your heart? Could you dream despite not being able to sleep?
Will you believe even when hope seems to be in short supply? Can you help though your best seems like only a little part? Do you choose to forget the past but the lessons learned from it keep? If the answer is yes then may you find the answers to everything dare to try.

The same

I am who I am.
You are who you are.
There's some things that makes us
different yet even more which are the same.
Let's focus on those & not something else.
Working together is how we'll solve our
problem.
Separated people will go nowhere new, yet
united we can go far.
So much is at stake for all of us, it's more
than just a silly game.
We need improve the scene before things
get more out of control & end up worse.

Eclipse

We can hear a million songs but
none of them will mean anything
until the time is right. We can
feel the sand between our toes
yet not experience beach unless
play in the waves.
We watch the
sky but not see it's
full magnificence till see an
eclipse.
So let's keep our head
up with eyes fully open day or
night. & not be afraid to wade
into the saltwater knowing
after a while it can cause
strongest of craves.
Remembering that each in its
own way can make a smile spread
across our lips.

Mask

Will you please take off your mask & show me who you really are when nobody else is around. I know you have one cause I too wear one, we all do it's just the way world works nowadays. Some individuals have them to scare others off, others to make themselves appear different than they really are. Me, mine is since I feel like wouldn't be understood if let others really knew my heart so I pretend not to care when if anything I care to much. & there's always so something on my mind just rarely speak since don't think people want to hear it. Hiding behind a mask is easy it allows us to show what we want seen but only when we are looking at each other fully can we start to
understand what makes us the people that we are.

Ink blots

She held up ink blots & asked what I saw
then wrote down my responses. Is there a
right & wrong way to answer those
questions? I'm not sure just know what I saw.
I'd be willing to bet even people that
administer the test have thoughts of their
own on before being taught what they're
supposed to see. Who's to say what they
are supposed to be, my mind works
differently then others; that doesn't make
me crazy. Does it? Just because I don't think
the way others do, shouldn't mean they
should be able to label me. Perhaps they're
the crazy ones for be willing to surrender
their individuality.

I am

I am one who dances in the rain.
A soul that wanders when it can.
A individual who plays amongst the waves.
That'll continuously chase the sunset.
Dreamer that can rarely fall asleep.
Someone who won't stop even during the pain.
That'll make it make through with hard work & a plan.
A person who has a insatiable crave.
Who follows their heart & will protect those in it.
A spirit this world can't keep.

Help another soul

It was the middle of night as made my way
through a sleepy small town with nobody else in
sight just streetlight after streetlight on deserted
street. A soft rain fell upon it & myself as I
walked trying to find shelter before the winter
storm in nearby mountains made its way to me.
Not a sound could be heard not even my steps
on the road, only proof I was there was my cool
breathe in the damp air. With eyes open wide I
trekked hoping to see somewhere I could rest
even if was just an hour or two yet nothing
presented itself so I continued on. As time
passed big & fuller clouds made their descent
into the quite community with no place to hide I
was drenched in their contents. Making my
clothes stick to me and shoes plop in & out of
puddles yet my presence made no impact on the
rest my of surroundings. A heavy fog rolled in
making streetlights my only guides disappear
one by one until nothing but fog surrounded me
as well in the distance. I tried to go faster yet the
now freezing air had made its way into my chest
made it impossible for me to, with every step I
felt weaker silently gasping for life. After what
felt like an eternity I reached a streetlight,

beneath it I saw woman standing there with her hand stretched out for mine. In a whisper she said do you want to come with me, my eyes opened as much as they could taking in the sight,despite standing under the illuminated light around her no shadow was cast. With a trembling voice I spoke saying what's happening,smiling she responded I'm just trying to help another soul make it through.

Anyone can love a rose. Or wish up a dandelion.
Yet only a certain person can care for a weed. A
rose will catch your eye with her color. The
dandelion with his magic. The weed with its
character. So is the life of a plant. Thus if you
ask me of three. Which of these I could be if had
to choose. All are special in creation. the answer
is simple indeed. I am who I am without
vibrance or mystical power.though I am part of
what makes though I am part of what makes the
world scenic. A uniquely designed part of its
feature. Being someone I'm not I can't.So for I
my choice the weed is me.

www.ingramcontent.com/pod-product-compliance
Lightning Source LLC
Chambersburg PA
CBHW071255140726
47996CB00007B/2855